Love
and
Longing
in the Age of
Chivalry

Love and Longing in the Age of Chivalry

Written and Compiled by

Martha Yeilding Scribner

RUTLEDGE HILL PRESS®

Nashville, Tennessee

Published by Rutledge Hill Press, Inc.,
211 Seventh Avenue North, Nashville, Tennessee 37219.
Distributed in Canada by H. B. Fenn & Company, Ltd.,
34 Nixon Road, Bolton, Ontario L7E 1W2.
Distributed in Australia by Five Mile Press Pty, Ltd.,
22 Summit Road, Noble Park, Victoria 3174.
Distributed in New Zealand by Tandem Press,
2 Rugby Road, Birkenhead, Auckland 10.
Distributed in the United Kingdom by Verulam Publishing, Ltd.,
152a Park Street Lane, Park Street, St. Albans, Hertfordshire AL2 2AU.

Design & composition by Gore Studio, Inc.

Library of Congress Cataloging-in-Publication Data

Love and longing in the age of chivalry / written and compiled by
    Martha Yeilding Scribner.
        p.   cm.
    ISBN 1-55853-672-8
    1. Love—Quotations, maxims, etc.   2. Courtly love—Quotations,
maxims, etc.   I. Scribner, Martha Yeilding, 1964–
PN6084.L6L5835   1998
302.3—dc21
                                                                98-29772
                                                                    CIP

Love
and
Longing
in the Age of
Chivalry

H, MY GOOD AND longed-for beloved, with well-formed figure sweet and slender, with fresh, pretty colored skin, whom God made with his own hands! Always I have desired you, and no one else pleases me— I want no other love.

—*Bernard de Ventadour*

ANYONE WHO HAS A beautiful woman for his wife or lover ought to be the better for it, for it cannot be right that she should love him after he has lost his fame and his worth.... Now more than ever it is of the first importance that your worth should increase!... Now you must not idle your time away, but you must frequent the tournaments, engage in combat, joust hard, whatever it costs you!

—*Chrétien de Troyes*

With you I should love to live, with you be ready to die.

—*Horace*

All other things, to their destruction draw,
Only our love hath no decay;
This, no tomorrow hath, nor yesterday,
Running, it never runs from us away,
But truly keeps his first, last, everlasting day.

—*John Donne*

If ever I kill my selfe for love, it shall be with a sigh, not with a sworde.

—*John Lyly*

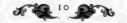

Our state cannot be sever'd; we are one,
One flesh; to lose thee were to lose myself.

—*John Milton*

For in my mind, of all mankind
I love but you alone.

—*Anonymous, "The Nut-Brown Maid"*

I was more true to Love than
Love to me.

—*Anonymous, John Dowland,*
The First Book of
Songs or Airs

11

ER TENDER ARMS, her back full
straight and soft,
Her slender flanks, all fleshly,
smooth, and white
Now he began to stroke, and blessed full oft
Her snowy throat, her breasts full round and light,
Thus in this heaven taking his delight;
And many thousand times he kissed her too,
Scarcely—from joy—knowing that next to do.

Of all the joys they had, one of the least
Is out of my capacity to say;
But you, if you have tasted such a feast,
Judge of their gladness, their sweet amorous play;
I can say nothing more than these two

That night, between certainty and dread,
Began to learn Love's power and worthiness.
Away, foul danger, and away, you fear,
And in this heavenly rapture let them dwell,
That is more lovely than my tongue can tell.

—*Chaucer,* Troylus and Criseyde,
Book III, ll 1226—1407

The Rules of Love

Andreas Capellanus

THESE RULES...*the Briton brought back with him on behalf of the King of Love to the lady for whose sake he endured many perils....When she was convinced of the complete faithfulness of this knight and understood better how boldly he had*

striven, she rewarded him with her love.
Then she called together a court of a
great many ladies and knights and laid
before them these rules of Love, and bade
every lover keep them faithfully under
threat of punishment by the King of
Love. These laws the whole court received
in their entirety and promised forever to
obey in order to avoid punishment by
Love. Every person who had been sum-
moned...gave them out to all lovers in
all parts of the world.

Marriage is no real excuse
for not loving.

❧

He who is not jealous cannot love.

❧

No one can be bound
by a double love.

❧

It is well known that love is always
increasing or decreasing.

❧

That which a lover takes against the
will of his beloved has no relish.

When one lover dies,
a widowhood of two years is
required of the survivor.

No one should be deprived of love
without the very best of reasons.

Love is always a stranger
in the home of avarice.

It is not proper to love any woman
whom one would be ashamed
to seek to marry.

A true lover does not desire to embrace
in love anyone except his beloved.

When made public love rarely endures.

The easy attainment of love
makes it of little value;
difficulty of attainment makes it prized.

A true lover thinks there is no happiness
except in pleasing his beloved.

A lover can never have enough
of the solaces of his beloved.

18

Love can deny
nothing to love.

A true lover would rather be
deprived of all his money and of everything
that the human mind can imagine as indispens-
able to life rather than be without love,
either hoped for or obtained.

Love is always an exile where
avarice holds its dwelling.

A person who cannot keep a secret
can never be a lover.

Love never stands still;
it always increases—or diminishes.

When made public love rarely endures.

Every lover regularly turns pale in
the presence of his beloved.

When a love suddenly
catches sight of his beloved
his heart palpitates.

A new love puts to flight an old one.

Good character alone makes
any man worthy of love.

A man in love is always apprehensive.

If love diminishes, it quickly fails
and rarely revives.

❦

Real jealousy always increases
the feeling of love.

❦

Jealousy, and
therefore love, are increased when
one suspects his beloved.

He whom the thought of love vexes
eats and sleeps very little.

Every action of a lover terminates
with the thought of the loved one.

A true lover considers
nothing good except what he thinks
will please his beloved.

A true lover is enthralled with the perpetual
image of his ladylove, which never at any
moment departs from his mind.

A true lover is continually
and without interruption obsessed by
the image of his beloved.

A love that has once been
rendered common and commonplace
never as a rule endures very long.

Too great prodigality of favors is
not advisable, for a lover who is wearied with
a superabundance of pleasure is generally
as a rule disinclined to love.

Courtly Love

❧——❧

OVE IS A CERTAIN inborn suffering derived from the sight of and excessive meditation upon the beauty of the opposite sex, which causes each one to wish above all things the embraces of the other and by common desire to carry out all of love's precepts in the other's embrace.

—*Andreas Capellanus*

Everyone wants to be in love, *but love is not a simple matter. When we are in love, we are ecstatic one moment and miserable the next. Often we rush into love, and we confuse it with physical pleasure.*

In the Middle Ages, people thought of love in a totally different way than we do. They developed a code of chivalry that included what was called Courtly Love. In this code a knight swore to protect and defend the one-and-only lady he adored. He would proudly wear her favor—a scarf or some love token—on the jousting field and into battle. He dedicated his victories to her honor, and he pledged to remember her name even after death.

The code of Courtly Love said that unattainable love was much more romantic than love that was easily obtained. Love was not considered an important reason for getting married because marriages were arranged for political gain or higher social status. In fact, some thought you could not love your spouse, because True Love could only exist between people who could not be together.

We appreciate love more when we have to wait for it, or even fight for it. Today it may be rare to experience this kind of love, but our idea of romance comes from this medieval attitude toward love. What woman does not dream of a handsome knight in shining armor coming to rescue her? Is there a man who does not want that chivalric combination of courage, strength, and daring to fight for his lady? When we dream of pure love, we imagine a consuming passion that cannot be denied despite the consequences.

Nobles, knights, and ladies at court constantly debated the nature of True Love. Queen Eleanor of Aquitaine even established a Court of Love to resolve romantic disputes. Love became an art, and courts of

love made up rules about how to conduct a love affair. These rules explained how to flirt, how to win someone's love, or how get a lover's attention. In the medieval world of battles and wars, these rules taught knights how to act like gentlemen and how to adore women. The rules of romance, or courtly love, called for knights to perform heroic deeds to gain the attention and admiration of their ladyloves. They rescued their lovers from evil foes, they went on dangerous quests, and they killed dragons.

The court entertainers, or troubadours, sang of knightly adventures filled with magic and wonder, and they created some of the most touching love stories of all time. These passionate tales inspire us to seek True Love, and they remind us not to take love for granted. There are still dragons to be slain and fair damsels to be rescued. Only those who are courageous and daring enough to recognize them can truly love.

HEN A MAN sees a woman worthy of love, and with a pleasing figure, he immediately begins to desire her in his heart, and the more he thinks about her the more he burns with love, until she fills his mind the whole time.

—*Andreas Capellanus*

Love is leche of lyf, and next owre lorde selue,
And also the graith gate that goth in-to heuene.

—*William Langland*

Never love unless you can
Bear with all the faults of man.

—*Campion*

Now it is the effect of love that a true lover
cannot be degraded with any avarice.
Love causes a rough and uncouth man to
be distinguished for his handsomeness; it
can endow a man even of the humblest birth
with nobility of character; it blesses the
proud with humility.

—*Andreas Capellanus*

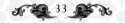

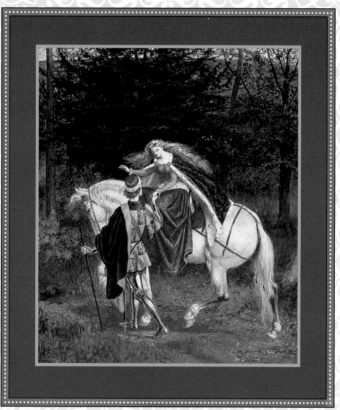

If I knew how to cast spells on people,

My enemies would be children,

So that no one could ever discover

Or tell a thing that could do us harm.

Then I know that I would see that most lovely lady,

And her beautiful eyes and her fresh complexion,

And I would kiss her on the mouth again and again,

So that the mark of it would show for a month.

I would like well to find her alone,

While she slept, or made semblance of it,

So that I could steal a sweet kiss from her,

Since I am too unworthy to ask for one.

By God, my lady, we accomplish little of love!

—*Bernard de Ventadour*

Love adorns a man with the virtue of chastity, because he who shines with the light of one love can hardly think of embracing another woman, even a beautiful one. For when he thinks deeply of his beloved the sight of any other woman seems to his mind rough and rude.

—*Andreas Capellanus*

Love regularly leaves it to the choice of each woman either to love or not, as she may wish, the person who asks for her love.

—*Andreas Capellanus*

I DO NOT SING for a bird
or a flower,
Nor for snow nor for ice,
Nor even for cold or warmth,
Nor for the return of the green
to the meadows;
Nor for any other pleasure
Do I sing, nor have I ever sung,
But for my lady for whom
I long,
For she is the fairest in
the world.

—*Geoffrey Chaucer*

BE LOYAL OF hand and mouth, and serve every man as best you may. Seek the fellowship of good men; hearken to their words and remember them. Be humble and courteous where'er you go, boasting not nor talking overmuch, neither be dumb altogether. Look to it that no lady or damsel be in reproach through your default, nor any woman of whatsoe'er quality. And if you fall into company where men speak disworshipfully of any woman, show by gracious words that it pleaseth you not, and depart.

—*Le Petit Jehan de Saintre*

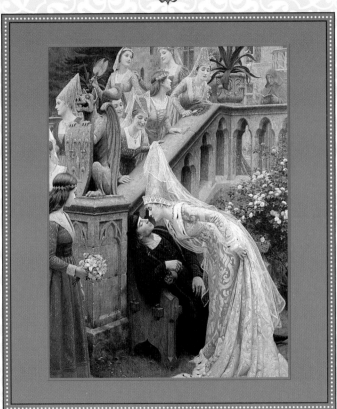

KNIGHTS WHO seek for honor,
   you should make sure
Of serving when you're armed
   ladies of worth:
   If you wish to use your time
In knights' ways, with honor,
Pay court to fairest women.

Your courage should be as high as you bear your shield;
You should be polished, bold, blithe and gentle
Serve knighthood with all your skill
And be glad, set love high,
Thus shall you win high praises.
Think now of the greetings of great ladies,
How sweet they make the life of their dear friends.
He who wins ladies' greetings
Wins honor, his desire;
His joy is all the sweeter.

—*Ulrich von Lichtenstein*

OME LIVE

with me, and be my love,

And we will some new pleasures prove

Of golden sands, and crystal brooks,

With silken lines, and silver hooks.

—*John Donne*

 HERE THERE
is much love,
there are usually but
few freedoms.

—*Cervantes*

I wonder by my troth, what thou, and I
Did, till we lov'd? Were we not wean'd till then?
But suck'd on country pleasures, childishly?…

—*John Donne*

What sweet thoughts, what longing
led them to the woeful pass.

—*Dante Algheri*

For God sake hold your tongue,
and let me love.

—*John Donne*

She loved Right fro the firste sighte.

—*Chaucer*

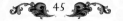

There is a lady sweet and kind,
Was ne'er face so pleased my mind;
I did but see her passing by,
And yet I love her till I die.

—*Anonymous,*
   Thomas Ford, Music of Sundry Kinds

See golden days, fruitful of golden deeds,
With Joy and Love triumphing.

—*John Milton*

WICE OR THRICE

had I loved thee

Before I knew thy face or name,

So in a voice, so in a shapeless flame,

Angels affect us oft, and

worshipped be.

—*John Donne*

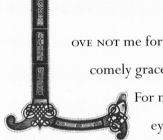

ove not me for

comely grace,

For my pleasing

eye or face,

Nor for any outward part,

No, nor for a constant heart.

—*Anonymous, John Wibye,*
Second Set of Madrigals

Forbidden Love

RIEND," she said, "now I entreat you, and warn you most urgently, that you do not reveal our love to anyone! And I shall tell you the reason for this: If our love is made known, you will have lost me forever; you will never be able to see me again, or have possession of my body."

—*Marie de France,*
Lanval, *ll 143-150*

AT ITS HEART, *courtly love was forbidden love—a bittersweet obsession. Lords and ladies of court were fascinated with the idea that love strikes wherever it wants. When two lovers could not consummate their love because they came from different classes, were married to someone else, or were forbidden by their families, they kept their love secret. This secret, impossible love was an engrossing passion nourished by its own difficulties. A true lover adored the one he could never have.*

> *This love wounds my heart so gently with its sweet savour: I die of grief a hundred times a day, and revive a hundred times with joy. (Bernard de Ventadour)*

> *When secret lovers adored each other, their rendezvous would be sensual and precious. The romance and excitement were heightened by the fear of discovery. Romance*

meant a furtive kiss or a secret meeting in a dark alcove. However, love was not always returned, and a lover some-times had to love from afar. When love was not welcome, the true lover persisted, never abandoning hope.

She may never give me all her love, nor would it be fitting, but if it pleased her to show me some kindness, I would swear to her on my faith that the favour she showed me should never be known through me; lest I please her, for I am at her mercy; if it please her to kill me, I complain not at all. (Bernard de Ventadour)

Forbidden love was a popular subject for the songs and tales performed at medieval courts. Troubadours sang of lovers gazing at each other across a bed of roses or about the agony of being in the same room without being able to touch each other.

Under the pretense of study, we gave ourselves entirely to love. More were the kisses than the learned opinions. No stage of love escaped our desires. If love could invent some new manner, we tried these too.

—*Abelard*

Love comes to an end after it has been openly revealed and made known to men.

—*Andreas Capellanus*

OVE IS said to improve if the lovers can only enjoy the sight of one another and come together infrequently and with difficulty; and in fact the greater the difficulty in standing before one another and embracing one another, the greater the longing, and the more the desire for love grows. . . . Love is usually intensified if you have gone away, or are about to go away, and also by the tirades and floggings that lovers endure from their parents.

—*Andreas Capellanus*

It would be a shame for such a beautiful woman not to have a lover! What would become of her finer qualities if she didn't nourish them by a secret love?

—*Marie de France*

Would God the night might never yield
    to morn,
And that my love might leave me not forlorn,
And that the watcher ne'er might see the dawn.
Ah God, ah God, the dawn, how soon it comes!

—*Anonymous*

 OME LIVE with me

and be my love;

And we will all the pleasures prove

That valleys, groves, hills, and fields,

Woods or steepy mountain yields.

—*Christopher Marlowe*

Live while ye may,
Yet happy couple.

—*John Milton*

Love is a thing as any
spirit free.

—*Chaucer*

Our two souls therefore which are one,
Though I must go, endure not yet
A breach, but an expansion,
Like gold to airy thinness beat.

—John Donne

The heart has its reasons which reason
knows nothing of.

—Blaise Pascal

Who can give law to lovers? Love is a greater law to itself.

—*Boëthius*

No one should be prevented from loving except by reason of his own death.

—*Andreas Capellanus*

For ever of love the siknesse
Is meynd with swete and bitternesse.

—*Chaucer*

I am desirous of a lady to whom I dare
not tell my wish, but when I look on her
face I am altogether bewildered. And shall I
ever have courage to dare to tell her she
may take me as her servant, since I dare not
beg for mercy from her?

—*Jaufre Rudel*

Love is a torment of the mind,
A tempest everlasting;
And Jove hath made it of a kind
Not well, nor full nor fasting.

—*Samuel Daniel*

Love, which is quickly kindled in the gentle heart, seized this man for the fair form that was taken from me, and the manner still hurts me. Love, which absolves no beloved one from loving, seized me so strongly with his charm that, as thou seest, it does not leave me yet.

—*Dante Algheri*

Both might and malice, deceyte and treacherye, all periurye, any impietie may lawfully be committed in love, which is lawlesse.

—*John Lyly*

Love, that all gentle hearts
so quickly know.

—*Dante Algheri*

It is impossible to love and
to be wise.

—*Francis Bacon*

Far worse it is to lose than
never to have tasted bliss.

—*Giambattista Guarnini*

Where both deliberate the
  love is slight:
Who ever lov'd that lov'd not
  at first sight?

—*Christopher Marlowe*

To live without love is a
  token of folly.

—*John Lyly*

Though the beginning of love brings delight, the ende bringeth destruction.

—*John Lyly*

I am two fools, I know
For loving, and for saying so
In whining poetry.

—*John Donne*

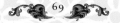

hail wedded love,
    mysterious law, true source
Of human offspring.

        —John Milton

harmony is pure love,
for love is complete agreement.

        —Lope de Vega

Remember the old saying,
"Faint heart ne'er won fair lady."

        —Miguel de Cervantes

Rebel and Atheist too,
    why murmur I
As though I felt the worst
    that love could do?

—John Donne

As love knoweth no lawes, so it
regardeth no conditions.

—John Lyly

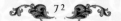

Love hath made wise men become fools, learned men ignorant, strong men weak.

—*John Florio*

Love is the tyrant of the heart.

—*John Ford*

Marriages are made in heaven and consummated on earth.

—*John Lyly*

You must as well love to live as live to love.

—*George Pettie*

Troubadours

*Tales of Passion
and Pleasure*

LAS, I THOUGHT I knew
so much
Of love, and yet I know
so little!
For I cannot stop myself
loving her
From whom I shall never have joy.
My whole heart, and all of me
from myself
She has taken, and her own self,
and all the world,
For when she took herself from me,
she left me nothing
But desire and a yearning heart.

—*Bernard de Ventadour*

KNIGHTHOOD WAS *about battle and bloodshed, horses and weapons, courage in combat, and fealty to a lord—until the twelfth century when troubadours in southern France turned their attention away from warfare and began to sing of love. Medieval audiences became obsessed with romantic stories of famous knights and virtuous maidens. The troubadours' songs became so popular that the code of courtly love developed and spread from the royal palaces of France to the courts and even the alehouses of England and Germany.*

A troubadour was a traveling minstrel or court musician who entertained royalty and commoners alike with poetry, music, and tales of adventure and love. Although they sang many tunes about war and politics, troubadours were at their best in the realm of romance.

A troubadour had to be educated, witty, charming,

and clever. Some moved from village to village, singing lusty ballads for whomever would listen. Others were sophisticated courtiers who composed passionate love songs for ladies and complex political ballads for noblemen.

The romantic accounts of star-crossed lovers sung by troubadours transformed savage warriors into gentlemanly knights and placed women on pedestals of perfection and beauty. Troubadours portrayed knights as noble, godly, and brave and described their daring quests through which they proved their love.

A troubadour would praise his beloved as being physically and morally perfect, would proclaim that her beauty illuminated the night, and would tell how her presence could heal the sick and cheer the sad. He would lament that separation from her was worse than death and vowed that if she did not love him in return, his passion would destroy him because he would not be able to eat, sleep, or sing.

Whoever can find a constant lover, he must love her and serve her to the utmost, and be completely at her will….Love granted [Guigemar] courage, so that he revealed to her his heart's desire. "Lady," said he, "I will die for your love. My heart is in agony from it, and if you are unwilling to heal me, then it will be the death of me in the end. I require of you your love; fair one, do not deny me!"

—*Marie de France,* Guigemar, *ll 493-506*

I F HE DESIRES my love,
damsel, he must show
A bold face, and be gay
and full of worth,
Frank and humble, not striving with any man,
And have a courteous reply for everyone;
For I don't want a proud or cruel man
Through whom my worth will be
decreased or lost,
But one who's frank and fair, discreet
and amorous:
If he wants me to treat him kindly, let him
listen to my words.

—*Anonymous female troubadour*

You cannot love bad men,
because Love's precept forbids that;
it follows then that you must give your
love only to good men.

—*Andreas Capellanus*

And if my homage she'd receive,
My wooing and my service true—
The sleepless nights I have been through,
The grief I bear from morn till eve,
Could never take me from her sight;
I'd be a slave unto delight,
All burdens I would gladly bear
And for my heart's grief I'd not care.

—*Guiraut de Bornelh*

Every day I improve and grow better,
For I serve and adore the noblest lady
In the world—and I declare it openly.
I am hers from head to foot;
And, even if the cold winds blow,
...And if she does not heal my suffering
With a kiss before the end of the year
She will murder me and damn herself.
Yet for all the suffering I endure
I do not renounce sweet love.

—*Arnaut Daniel*

 GREAT EXCESS of lust prevents love, because there are those who are so enslaved to their sensual desires that they cannot be bound in the nets of love; men who, after they have set their minds on one woman, or even taken their enjoyment with her, when they afterwards see another woman, immediately desire her embraces, and then are oblivious to the indulgences they received from their first love, and are not grateful for

them. Men like this lust after every woman they see indiscriminately. The love of such men is like that of a shameless dog. In fact I believe they should be compared to asses; for they are moved only by those qualities which show men to be just the same as the other beasts, and not by those true qualities which set us apart from animals by the difference of reason.

—*Andreas Capellanus*

Noble lady I ask of you
To take me as your servitor;
I'll serve you as I would my lord
Whatever my reward shall be.
Look, I am here at your command,
You who are noble, gay and kind
You are no bear or lion's whelp
Who'll kill me if I yield to you.

—*Bernard de Ventadour*

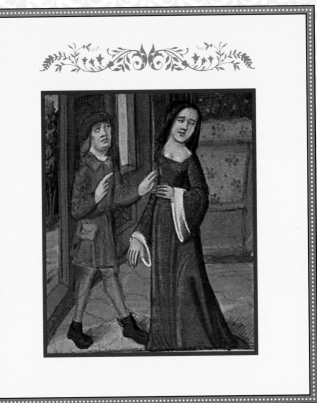

All men know that if one gets easily what he desires he holds it cheap and what formerly he longed for with his whole heart he now considers worthless.

—*Andreas Capellanus*

Were all the world mine
From the sea to the Rhine
I'd give it all away
If England's Queen lay
In my arms.

—*Bernard de Ventadour,
to honor Queen Eleanor of Aquitaine*

I am greatly surprised that you wish me to apply the term 'love' to the marital affection which husband and wife are expected to feel for each other after marriage, since everybody knows that love can have no place between husband and wife. They may be bound to each other by a great and immoderate affection, but their feeling cannot take the place of love, because it cannot fit under the true definition of love. For what is love but an inordinate desire to receive passionately a furtive and hidden embrace? But what embrace between husband and wife can be furtive?

—*Andreas Capellanus*

For the wise and well-taught lover, when conversing for the first time with a lady whom he has not previously known, should not ask in specific words for gifts of love, but he should try hard to give a hint to the lady he loves, and should show himself pleasant and courteous in all that he says; then he should be careful to act in such a way that his deeds praise him truly to his love, even when he is absent.

—*Andreas Capellanus*

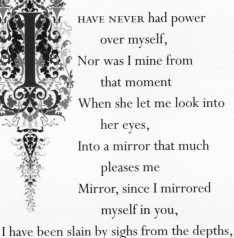

HAVE NEVER had power
        over myself,
Nor was I mine from
        that moment
When she let me look into
        her eyes,
Into a mirror that much
        pleases me
Mirror, since I mirrored
        myself in you,
I have been slain by sighs from the depths,
And thus I was lost, just as
The fair Narcissus lost himself in the pool.

—*Bernard de Ventadour*

It is the pure love which binds together the hearts of two lovers with every feeling of delight. This kind consists in the contemplation of the mind and the affections of the heart; it goes as far as the kiss and the embrace and the modest contact with the nude lover, omitting the final solace, for that is not permitted to those who wish to love purely.

—*Andreas Capellanus*

SWEET LADY, that ring

That you gave me gives me

great comfort

For by it my sorrow is lessened

And, when I look on it, I am more lighthearted

Than a starling;

And for your sake I am so brave,

I am not afraid that either lance nor arrow

Can do me harm, nor steel nor iron.

But on the other hand, I am in deeper despair

Through too much loving

Than a ship when it is tossed on the sea

Distressed by waves and winds,

So terribly do my thoughts torment me.

—Giraut de Borneil

Too many opportunities for exchanging solaces, too many opportunities of seeing the loved one, too much chance to talk to each other all decrease love.

—*Andreas Capellanus*

Love and War are the same thing, and stratagems and policy are as allowable in the one as in the other.

—*Miguel de Cervantes*

Love is no longer love when it is without arrows and without fire.

—*Montaigne*

To be able to say how much you love is to love but little.

—*Petrarch*

He loves too much that dies for love.

—*Randle Cotgrave*

Ah, what is love? It is a pretty thing,
as sweet unto a shepherd as a king.

—*Robert Greene*

Old love is little worth when new is more prefard.

—*Edmund Spencer*

Love can finde entrance, not only into an open Heart; but also into a Heart well fortified, if watch be not well kept.

—*Francis Bacon*

Lancelot
and
Guinevere

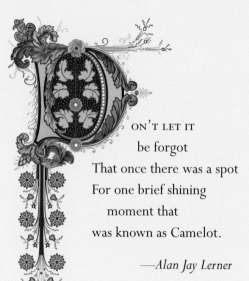

Don't let it
be forgot
That once there was a spot
For one brief shining
moment that
was known as Camelot.

—*Alan Jay Lerner*

The troubadours' *favorite topics came from Celtic legends. They sang of tragic lovers like Troylus and Criseyde, Trisam and Isolde, and the most heart-wrenching of all love affairs, that of Lancelot and Guinevere.*

There are many versions of the story of Lancelot, but the oldest describes him as the son of Ban, king of Gomeret. When Ban was killed, the Lady of the Lake stole the child Lancelot from his mother, Elaine, and reared him herself. The Lady was an otherworldly woman with magical powers, and by the time she sent him to King Arthur's court to be knighted, Lancelot had been taught to be noble, brave, courteous, and a true knight. He had many adventures on his journey to Arthur's court, defeating evil foes, rescuing maidens, and honing his knightly skills. When he reached Arthur, Lancelot was reputed to be the most virturous and brave knight in Christendom.

Arthur knighted the young Lancelot and made him Queen Guinevere's champion. The two fell hopelessly in love at first sight, and Lancelot rescued Guinevere from many dangers. Out of respect for the king, they resisted their attraction as long as they could, but their love for each other was overwhelming. The two were destined to love but never to be together.

With a heavy conscience, Lancelot began his quest for the Holy Grail and then realized that his adulterous affair with the queen had tarnished his soul. No longer the most perfect and true knight in the kingdom, he was forbidden the discovery of the Grail. He did penance for his sin and was allowed to reach the Grail castle, but he never glimpsed the holy cup itself.

On his return to Camelot, Lancelot renewed his affair with the queen. The lovers become careless and were exposed by Mordred, Arthur's evil son. Lancelot escaped and was exiled, but the law dictated that Guinevere be burned at the stake. Despite his feelings for her, Arthur could not place himself above the law to save his queen. At the last minute, Guinevere's loyal champion Lancelot defied all to rescue his lover from the burning stake.

Lancelot and Guinevere shared a rare and irresistible passion, and although they fought it, their adulterous— and treasonous—love tore Camelot in two and destroyed Arthur's dream of unity, peace, and justice. Guinevere spent the rest of her life in a convent doing penance for her sin. Lancelot lost his wits and wandered in the woods while Camelot slowly disintegrated. The love story of Lancelot and Guinevere is unforgettable because of the strength of their love and its tragic end. True love, however, conquers all, and legend has it that once the two lovers renounced their worldly sins they were united in spirit for eternity.

Lancelot, upon seeing Guinevere:

The knight at the window recognized that it was the Queen. As long as she remained in his sight, he continued to gaze at her most attentively, and with delight. But when he could see her no longer, he wanted to fling himself out of the window and shatter his body on the ground below. He was already halfway out of the window when my lord Sir Gawain spotted him and pulled him back in.

—Chrétien de Troyes, Lancelot

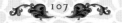

HEN LANCELOT perceived the
Queen leaning towards the
window at the massive iron
grille, he greeted her in a low
voice. The Queen returned his
greeting, for she greatly
desired him, as he did her. In
their words was nothing base
or disagreeable, on the con-
trary. They drew as close to one another as they could,
and held each other's hands. They were maddened
beyond endurance at not being able to come together,
and they cursed the iron bars. But Lancelot boasted
that if the Queen consented, he would enter the cham-
ber; it was not the bars of the window that were pre-
venting him. The Queen said, "Do you not see how
solid these bars are—how could you break them, or

even bend them?" "My lady," answered Lancelot, "do
not think of that! The iron is worthless as far as I am
concerned. Nothing will stop me from coming in to
you, but you yourself. If you grant your permission,
the way is free. But if you do not wish it, then the path
is so full of obstacles that I shall never be able to pass."
"As for me, I desire it," said the Queen. "My wishes
will never prevent you."

The knight prepared himself to attack the window.
He grasped the bars, heaved and pulled them down
until he had quickly bent them all and could force
them out of their sockets. But the iron was so sharp
that it pierced the tip of one finger to the bone, and
sliced through another at the first joint. But his
preoccupation was so intense that he felt no pain
from these wounds, nor did he notice the blood which
poured from them.

All ye that be lovers call unto your remem-brance the month of May, like as did Queen Guine-vere, for whom I make here a little mention, that while she lived she was a true lover, and therefore she had a good end.

—*Sir Thomas Malory,*
    Le Morte d'Arthur,
    bk. XVIII, ch. 25

Lancelot upon discovering Guinevere's comb:

He began to adore the hairs; a hundred thousand times he touched them to his eyes, his mouth, his forehead, and his cheeks. His joy was made manifest in every way, and he thought himself rich and happy indeed. He placed the hairs in his breast, close to his heart, between the shirt and the skin. He would not exchange them for a cartload of emeralds and carbuncles.

—*Chrétien de Troyes*, Lancelot

The month of May was come, when every lusty heart beginneth to blossom, and to bring forth fruit; for like as herbs and trees bring forth fruit and flourish in May, in likewise every lusty heart that is in any manner a lover, springeth and flour-isheth in lusty deeds. For it giveth unto all lovers courage, that lusty month of May.

—*Sir Thomas Malory*, Le Morte d'Arthur, *bk. xviii, ch. 25*

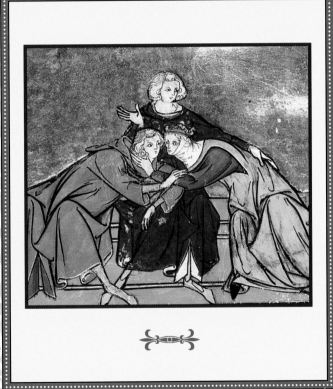

For as well as I have loved thee heretofore, mine heart will not serve now to see thee; for through thee and me is the flower of kings and knights destroyed.

—*Sir Thomas Malory,* Le Morte d'Arthur, *bk. XXI, ch. 9*

Then Sir Launcelot saw her visage, but he wept not greatly, but sighed!

—*Sir Thomas Malory,* Le Morte d'Arthur, *bk. XXI, ch. 11*

THEIR HIGH FEAST was love,

who gilded all their joys.

Love brought them as

homage the Round Table and all its

company a thousand times a day.

What better food could they have for

body or soul?

What else should they be needing?

They had what they were meant to have.

They had reached the goal of their desire.

—*Gottfried von Strassburg,*
Tristram and Isolde

LOVE AIMED WELL when he shot his arrow into her heart— often she grew pale and broke into a sweat; in spite of herself she was forced to love.

—*Chrétien de Troyes*, Cliges

The Queen stretched out her arms to him and embraced him; she pressed him to her breast, and then drew him into the bed beside her. She made him the most beautiful welcome that anyone could do who was inspired by love in their heart. Indeed, she felt for him great love, but Lancelot loved her a thousand times more. Love had taken root in his heart so completely, that there was scarcely any left over for other hearts. Now Lancelot had everything he desired; the queen wished him to stay beside her and enjoy her; he held her in his arms and she held him in hers.

—*Chrétien de Troyes,* Lancelot

Lancelot knew such joy, such pleasure the night long, that he could hardly bear the coming of day when he had to leave his lover's bed. Wrenching himself away was crucifixion. Torn with misery he bowed to her bed as if it were an altar; and left the room.

—*Chrétien de Troyes,* Lancelot

Who loves well is slow to forget.
(Qui bien aime a tard oublie.)

—*Chaucer*

Love lodged in a woman's breast
Is but a guest.

—*Sir Henry Wotton*

For love is blynd.

—*Chaucer*

AND FRO HER look in him
began to grow
Such great desire and passionate affection
That in the bottom of his heart did show
An image deeply fixed of her impression.
And though at first he'd gazed around the room,
His insolent horn began now in to shrink,
He scarcely knew whether to look or blink.

—*Chaucer,* Troilus and Criseyde,
Book I, ll 295-301

And I will make thee beds of roses
And a thousand fragrant posies.

—*Christopher Marlowe*

With a look his herte wex a-fire.

—*Chaucer*

Love hath so long possessed me
   for his own
And made his lordship so familiar.

—*Dante Algheri*

And from then on Love robbed him
of his sleep,
Made of his food his foe, and then his sorrow
Multiplied so that, if anyone took keep,
It showed in his complexion night
and morrow....

But the poor Troilus suffered such
great woe
That he went almost mad, for his fear went
That she already loved another so
That to his pains she'd be indifferent,
For which he felt his heart's blood
almost spent.

—*Chaucer,* Troilus and Criseyde,
Book I, ll 484-490, 498-504

Love is swift, sincere, pious, pleasant, gentle, strong, patient, faithful, prudent, long-suffering, manly and never seeking her own; for wheresoever a man seeketh his own, there he falleth from love.

—*Thomas á Kempis*

Love is the blossom where there blows
Every thing that lives or grows.

—*Giles Fletcher*

THROUGH THEIR kisses
and caresses they
experienced a joy
and wonder the equal
of which has never
been known or heard of.
But I shall be silent...for the
rarest and most delectable
pleasures are those which are
hinted at, but never told.

—*Chrétien de Troyes,* Lancelot

ACKNOWLEDGMENTS

Page 2: "La Belle Dame Sans Merci" by Sir Frank Dicksee (1853-1928) Robert Frederick, Ltd.; Page 6: Two lovers in a garden. Illustration from the Vaticinia for the days of the year. Abbey, Kremsmuenster, Austria. Photograph © by Erich Lessing/Art Resource, NY; Page 9: Lancelot fights the champions of the false Guinevere from *Le Roman de Lancelot du Lac,* northeastern France, early 14th century. The Pierpont Morgan Library, NY/Art Resource, NY; Page 19: May: Hawking. Playfair Book of Hours. France (Rouen), late 15th century. Victoria & Albert Museum, London/Art Resource, NY; Page 22: "La Belle Dame Sans Merci" by John William Waterhouse (1849-1917) Robert Frederick, Ltd.; Page 26: "Bitomart and Amoret" by Mary F. Raphael, Robert Frederick, Ltd.; Page 34: "La Belle Dame Sans Merci" by Walter Crane, Christopher Wood Gallery, London/The Bridgeman Art Library International; Page 39: Frederic Leighton (1830-96). Alain Chartier, 1903. Fine Art Photographic Library, London/Art Resource, NY; Page 40: "'God Speed'" by Edmund Blair Leighton (1853-1922) Robert Frederick, Ltd.; Page 44: "How Sir Gareth came to the presence of his lady, and how they took acquaintance, and of their love" by W. Russell Flint, illustration for *Le Morte Darthur* by Sir Thomas Malory; Page 48: "Hesperus" by Sir Joseph Noel Paton (1821-1901) Robert Frederick, Ltd.; Page 50: Gawain visiting the Daughter of King of Norgales, from *Le Roman de Lancelot du Lac,* northeastern France, early 14th century. The Pierpont Morgan Library, NY/Art Resource, NY; Page 56: Courtesy Library of Congress, Verner W. Clapp Fund; Page 63: Courtesy Library of Congress, Verner W. Clapp Fund; Page 67: "Emilia in her garden," Hours of the Duke of Burgundy (1454-55), Osterreichische Nationalbibliothek, Vienna, Austria/The Bridgeman Art Library International; Page 72: Courtesy Library of Congress, Verner W. Clapp Fund; Page 74: "The Minstrel's Lady" by George Sheridan Knowles (1863-1931) Robert Frederick, Ltd.; Page 82: Offering of the Heart. Tapestry from Arras, France, 15th century. Musee du Moyan Age (Cluny), Paris. Giraudon/Art Resource, NY; Page 87: Courtesy Library of Congress, Verner W. Clapp Fund; Page 92: "The Riven Shield" by Philip Richard Morris (1838-1902), Roy Miles Gallery, London/The Bridgeman Art Library International; Page 98: "They went into their country of Benoye, and lived there in great joy" by W. Russell Flint, illustration for *Le Morte Darthur* by Sir Thomas Malory; Page 100: "Lancelot and Guinevere" by Henry James Draper (1864-1920), Phillips, The International Fine Art Auctioneers, UK/The Bridgeman Art Library International; Page 106: Lancelot and Guinevere from *Lancelot du Lac,* c. 1470, Bibliotheque Nationale, Paris/The Bridgeman Art Library International; Page 113: First kiss of Lancelot and Guinevere from *Le Roman de Lancelot du Lac,* northeastern France, early 14th century. The Pierpont Morgan Library, NY/Art Resource, NY; Page 118: "How Sir Launcelot and his kinsmen rescued the queen from the fire" by W. Russell Flint, illustration for *Le Morte Darthur* by Sir Thomas Malory; Page 122: Abelard and Heloise, Miniature from royal manuscript, British Library, London/Art Resource, NY; Page 127: "They fought for the love of one lady, and ever she lay on the walls and beheld them," by W. Russell Flint, illustration for *Le Morte Darthur* by Sir Thomas Malory; Decorative art on pages 11, 13, 69, 95, and 112 courtesy of Library of Congress, Verner W. Clapp Fund.